BECOMING YOUR
BIRD'S
BEST FRIEND

BECOMING YOUR BIRD'S BEST FRIEND

BY BILL GUTMAN

ILLUSTRATED BY
ANNE CANEVARI GREEN

Pet Friends
The Millbrook Press
Brookfield, Connecticut

Published by The Millbrook Press, Inc.
2 Old New Milford Road
Brookfield, Connecticut 06804

Printed in the United States of America
5 4 3 2 1

Library of Congress Cataloging-in-Publication Data
Gutman, Bill.
Becoming your bird's best friend/by Bill Gutman
illustrated by Anne Canevari Green.
p. cm.—(Pet friends)
Includes bibliographical references (p.) and index.
Summary: Provides information about the physical and psychological
needs of pet birds, as well as about how to choose and
care for them as pets.
ISBN 1-56294-662-5 (lib. bdg.)
1. Cage birds—Juvenile literature. 2. Cage birds—Behavior—
Juvenile literature. [1. Birds as pets.] I. Green, Anne
Canevari, ill. II. Series: Gutman, Bill. Pet friends.
SF461.G87 1996
636.6'8—dc20   96-5188 CIP AC

The author would like to thank

Dr. Alan Peterson, DVM,

of Community Animal Hospital
in Poughkeepsie, New York,
for his careful reading of
the manuscript and his many
helpful comments and suggestions.

UNDERSTANDING YOUR PETS

Animals have always played a major role in people's lives. In earlier days, animals did a great deal of work. Oxen pulled the plows that tilled the fields. Horses provided transportation. Dogs were used to guard people and herds of cattle or flocks of sheep. Wherever there were humans, there were usually animals, too.

Today, animals are still a big part of many people's lives. Some still work. Others are kept in zoos or on game farms. And countless millions of animals are simply family pets.

There is much more to pet care than simple feeding and housing. Whether you have a dog, a cat, a bird, tropical fish, a hamster, a gerbil, a guinea pig, or even a horse or pony, you owe it to that animal to learn all you can about it. Obviously, animals can't tell you their feelings. You have to guess what they are thinking and feeling by the way they are acting—by their sounds, their movements, and by changes in their behavior.

This is very important if you want to have a happy, healthy pet who will live out its natural life span. The *Pet Friends* series will not only discuss basic animal care. It will also strive to show what your pet thinks and feels as it lives its life with you.

YOUR PET BIRD

Birds have been kept as pets for thousands of years. Everyone has seen pictures of a pirate captain on a ship with a big green parrot sitting on his shoulder. That is an image from the past. Today, bird keeping is a more popular hobby than ever before.

People keep pet birds for many different reasons. Some like to breed them because they enjoy watching a pair of birds raise a family. Others like to keep a single bird as a pet. A single bird can be a friend and companion for many years.

Some pet birds sing and make very pleasant chirping sounds. Others can talk. They imitate the human voice and other sounds in their home. Many birds will also shriek and squawk at times. To birds, these vocal sounds are natural. But you really have to love them to listen to that kind of noise.

A bird is a different kind of pet than a dog or cat. The most obvious difference is that it can fly. For this reason, a bird kept in a cage is in an unnatural situation. It wants to fly among the trees and be with other birds. Its natural instincts are to be part of a flock.

If you have a single pet bird, you and your family become its "flock." The bird will want to be part of the family, not left by itself in a separate room. It wants to see and hear what's going on and interact with its family/flock. Yet in many ways, it will still behave as if it were a bird in the wild.

As a bird owner, you must learn to understand these ways. Only you can provide the things that will make your bird happy and healthy. And the more you know about your bird, what it needs, and why it does the things it does, the better you will be able to give it the full life it deserves.

WHOEVER THOUGHT OF KEEPING PET BIRDS?

Birds first appeared on Earth some 150 million years ago. The earliest birds were prehistoric animals, like dinosaurs. It is thought that birds were first kept as pets by the Chinese. They began breeding pheasants thousands of years ago. The Alexandrine parakeet is named for the Roman general Alexander

the Great. These birds were kept as caged pets during the days of the Roman Empire.

The first parrot was seen in England in 1504. The English were pioneers in the field of aviculture. *Aviculture* is the name given to keeping and breeding birds. The Avicultural Society of England was formed in 1894, and the Avicultural Society of America began in 1927.

But it wasn't until the 1950s that birds really became popular as pets in the United States. Their popularity has grown ever since. Now there are millions of little parakeets, or budgerigars, kept in homes in the United States. There are also canaries, finches, cockatiels, lovebirds, conures, African gray parrots, Amazon parrots, cockatoos, and macaws.

Except for canaries and finches, all the others mentioned above are members of the parrot, or Psittacine, family. They can be identified by their hooked bills. All members of the parrot family are highly intelligent animals. In the wild they live in large flocks high in the trees. Most members of the parrot family mate with one other bird for life. They breed, search for food much of the time, and warn each other of danger.

The birds of the parrot family make the best pets. From the smallest "budgie" to the largest macaw, these birds can make loving companions. Most of them have long life spans. They can be taught to do tricks, and many of them can talk!

But it isn't always easy to have a great pet bird. It takes work, patience, and a lot of love. It also takes understanding. You must know what kind of bird you are getting and where it came from.

There are two basic ways a pet bird can find its way to your home. It can be either imported or domestically raised. Imported birds are brought into the United States and Canada from other countries. All species of parrots come from warm-weather climates such as Mexico, Central and South America, Africa, and Australia. No parrot lives naturally in the United States or Canada.

The importing of birds is now illegal in many places. Many birds are killed in the process of capturing a few. Some members of the parrot family are already extinct. Many others are endangered. That means that if they are not soon protected, they may also become extinct.

Domestically raised birds are bred in the country where they are to be sold. Many of these are hand-raised by the breeder and become tame very quickly. But any bird must be handled often and with love to remain tame. Birds have very long memories. Once they are mistreated they never forget. They may fear the person who mistreated them, or they may fear all people.

Without a doubt, it is best to get a bird that has been domestically raised. Not only will your bird be easier to tame, but more birds will remain in the wild, where the species can continue to breed and thrive. And buying domestically may help put the bird smugglers out of business.

HOW DO I FIND THE
RIGHT BIRD FOR ME?

One of the great attractions of pet birds are the sounds they make. All members of the parrot family, from budgies to macaws, have the ability to mimic the human voice. Some birds are better talkers than others. Even birds of the same species can vary greatly in their individual characteristics.

BUDGERIGARS (PARAKEETS)

Budgies are sweet little birds. They are about 7 inches (18 centimeters) long from the head to the tip of the long tail. In the wilds of Australia they are green with black bars on the wings and back. Bred in captivity, they come in all kinds of color combinations, from all yellow, to all white, to various mixtures of yellow, blue, white, green, and black.

As the bird matures, the small area just above the beak (called the *cere*) becomes blue in the male. In females it is brown or tan. Both males and females make equally good pets.

Budgies can live from eight to fifteen years, though many don't live past the age of five because of neglect and lack of exercise. As a rule, they are not noisy birds. They will chirp and whistle, and some will talk. Single birds are more likely to talk than two or more. But once a bird is talking, it will keep talking even with another bird in the cage.

Young budgies can be easily finger-tamed and will love to come out of the cage. Despite their small size, they can be affectionate companions.

COCKATIELS

Cockatiels also come from Australia. They are 10 to 13 inches (25 to 33 centimeters) long from the top of their crest to the tip of a long tail. They have a life span of fifteen to twenty-five years, so they will be with you for a long time.

Normal cockatiels are gray with orange cheek patches and some white on the wings. Lutino cockatiels are all white with possibly a bit of yellow wash. Pieds are mottled with white spots, while Pearls have a scalloped white-and-yellow pattern at the ends of their feathers.

In normal gray cockatiels, mature males (beginning at seven months) have a yellow-and-white head. The color spreads to some of the crest feathers. Females retain the gray head. Both males and females are gentle birds that make wonderful pets. Young birds are easily tamed.

Male cockatiels can become good talkers and whistlers. They sometimes tend to be more independent than the females. Some females will talk, but as a rule they are more loving and quiet.

LOVEBIRDS

Lovebirds are mischievous little birds, 5 to 7 inches (13 to 18 centimeters) long, with a life span of ten to fifteen years. They come in several varieties and colors. Some will talk, but not all. They are hardy and inexpensive. They love to shred paper and sometimes hide under it. Many people enjoy watching lovebirds in pairs because they often sit nuzzled together. But a single bird can be happy if you give it a great deal of attention.

THE LARGER PARROTS

A wide variety of midsize and larger parrots are kept as pets: conures, ring-necked parakeets, African gray and Amazon parrots, a large assortment of beautiful cockatoos, and both midsize and very large macaws, as well as a number of other lesser-known species.

Many of these birds are breathtakingly beautiful. The African grays and some of the Amazons (yellow napes, blue fronts, and Mexican double yellowheads) can be amazing talkers with humanlike voices and very large vocabularies.

But at the same time, these birds can be much harder to handle than budgies, lovebirds, or cockatiels. Some tend to be moody, especially when they reach maturity. This can take three

to five years, depending on the species. It is not uncommon to have a bird that is sweet for a few years, then suddenly changes, especially during the breeding season.

The larger birds can also be extremely noisy. The constant shrieking of an Amazon, cockatoo, or macaw can sometimes drive even real bird lovers to distraction. In addition, if you don't know how to handle your bird, you can get a very severe bite.

A larger parrot is not a good first bird for most people, and especially not for children. If a large parrot becomes a family pet, or if there has been a large parrot in the house for years, you should learn all you can about it. Until then, don't even try to handle it.

YOUR FIRST BIRD

It is always an exciting day when a new pet comes into the home. Whether it is a dog, cat, bird, or some other animal, everyone wants to gather around, touch, and play with the newest family member. But birds are not like other animals. When a new bird is brought into the home, there are certain things that should be done.

To begin with, the bird *must* be wanted. It can't be a matter of "let's get a bird and see how it works out." It is very difficult for some birds to be passed around from family to family. Birds have feelings, just as people and dogs do.

There is a lot more to keeping a pet bird than changing the food and water every day and cleaning the cage. And it all begins when you bring your bird home. With good care, birds are very hardy animals. But during the first few months in a new home birds can get sick easily.

What usually makes birds sick is stress. Stress is mental or physical tension. All of us have stress at some time. People who have a great deal of stress can get sick, too. It's very important to try to keep the stress level low for your new bird.

The best way to do this at the beginning is simply to not make a fuss over it. It needs quiet time. The bird doesn't know you yet, and touching and petting it will cause stress. You may be trying to show it that you love it, but the bird may still think your hand is going to harm it.

Speak to your bird quietly for a few minutes at a time. But don't have friends and neighbors over to gawk at it, making silly whistles and noises. And don't let anyone poke their fingers through the cage to try to touch it. They may mean well, but the bird won't understand.

No matter how it seems to act, nearly every bird coming to a new home for the first time is frightened. It doesn't know if it can trust these strange people. It doesn't know what other dangers may lurk in its new surroundings. The bird is under stress—don't make it worse.

Here are some other tips for bringing home a new bird:

1. Keep the room warm, maybe a bit warmer than usual. Make sure there are no cold drafts anywhere near the cage.

2. If at all possible, for at least the first week feed your bird the same food it had been eating before you got it.

3. Make sure the bird has ten to twelve hours of total quiet and darkness each day. You can cover the cage at night to block out sounds and light.

4. Unless the bird is already tame and wants companionship, do not try to handle it for the first few weeks. There will be plenty of time later.

5. Keep it in the cage. Don't let it out to fly around. Give it time to get used to its new home and family. Keep other pets away.

6. Try not to expose the bird to any sudden loud noises in the house.

Having a pet bird is a big responsibility. Most dogs have life spans of between eight and fifteen years. A pet parrot could stay in the family for twenty-five years or more. During its entire life it will need the same kind of loving care it needs at the beginning.

ONE OR TWO BIRDS?

Look at it from the bird's point of view. In the wild, birds live in large flocks. When a bird finds a mate they both stay within the flock. Birds in the wild never go off on their own. A bird kept mostly in a cage is already in an unnatural situation. A bird kept alone in a cage is in an even more unnatural situation.

If a bird has constant companionship from its "person" or family.... If it receives a great deal of attention and love.... If it is allowed to come out of its cage often and be with its family....

I'M SO LONELY EVEN **HE** LOOKS INTERESTING !

Then it won't be unhappy as a solitary bird. It can bond with its person and have the family as its flock.

But if you're at school for most of the day and your parents work, the bird will be alone for long hours at a time. If you go out on weekends and away on vacations, the bird will be lonely and unhappy no matter how many toys it has in its cage. In this situation, you should consider a second bird.

You don't have to get both birds at once. You can tame the first and get a second bird later. If you do this, you can easily have two loving and affectionate pets. And when you're not there, they will have each other.

WHERE'S THE DECORATOR AND THE CHEF?

Birds don't automatically want to be with people. Any bird would rather be up among the trees with its flock, looking for a mate and searching for a variety of foods.

You can't give a pet bird a healthy and happy life by just putting it in a cage and feeding it. There is a great deal more to bird keeping than that. The key is allowing the bird to follow its natural instincts whenever possible. That means giving it a chance to do similar things that it would do in the wild.

CAGES

The cage is going to be your bird's home for a good part of each day and you hope for many years. Depending on the cage you choose and how you fix it up, it can be a palace or it can be a prison. The first rule is to buy the largest cage you can afford that will fit in your home. You can't have a cage that's too big, but you can have a cage that's too small. As a rule, the cage should be at least large enough so that the bird can hold onto the

bars and flap its wings freely. Small canaries or budgies do fine in a standard-size cage, but a larger bird like an Amazon parrot, cockatoo, or macaw will need a much larger one.

Rectangular cages are best. The bird can move around more, and a small bird may actually be able to fly a bit. The bars should be close enough together so that the bird cannot poke its head through. This can lead to a serious injury.

PERCHES

The selection and placement of perches in a cage are very important. Remember, birds stand on perches twenty-four hours a day; they do not lie down to go to sleep. For birds to be comfortable, perches should not be so large that the bird's feet cannot grip them, and they should not be so small that the front and rear toes touch or overlap when the bird stands on them. It's best to provide a few different perches of varying shapes and sizes, so that your bird can stretch its feet and shift its weight around.

30

The perches should be far enough apart for the bird to move freely. If your bird has a long tail, it shouldn't rub on another perch or on the cage. Don't be disturbed if your bird chews its perches. This is natural—all birds chew to some degree. Hookbilled birds must chew to keep the upper half of their beak (called a *rhinotheca*) from becoming overgrown. If a perch becomes too chewed, replace it.

The best perches are natural ones from edible trees (since your birds will probably chew on them) such as maple, ash, eucalyptus, and fruit and nut trees. Some woods, such as black locust, cherry, and oak, can make your bird ill if it chews them. You can also buy natural wood perches at many pet stores.

If you cut your own perch, bake it in an oven at a low heat for thirty to forty-five minutes before using. This will kill any insects that may be lurking inside the wood.

TOYS

Toys serve more than one purpose in a bird's cage. They provide exercise, keep your bird from getting bored, and give it something else to chew. There are many bird toys on the market. Small birds like rings, swings, and small bells. Larger birds like wooden toys they can gnaw on and push around.

Toys for larger birds are made from hardwood, rawhide, lava rocks, and durable plastic. If you make your own toys, make sure the materials are not painted or stained and that they contain no harmful chemicals, especially lead.

Also make sure to use chains to suspend your toys. Never use a string or cord. It can easily become wrapped around your bird's foot, leg, or even its neck.

FOOD

You might think that a caged bird has an easy life. After all, it doesn't even have to hunt for its food. But the truth is that birds enjoy a good challenge. If you know a few basics, it's very easy to feed a bird and satisfy its natural instincts at the same time.

The first step is to provide the right kind of food. For years, it was thought that a good variety of seed was enough. Then it was learned that hookbills also need fruits and vegetables. The problem is that many birds pick a favorite food or seed and eat little else. As it turns out, this kind of feeding does not provide a balanced diet.

The best way to feed pet hookbills (from budgies to macaws) is to buy a commercial bird diet in the form of pellets. These diets are as close to a balanced diet for a bird as you can get. Birds who have been eating seeds may not like pellets at first. It may take a while to get them used to the new food. Birds raised on pellets eat them happily.

A bird eating only pellets can stay healthy for years. But even that isn't enough. In the wild, searching for food is a major activity that can take up a good part of the day. Birds enjoy opening up a new food with their beaks, holding it with their feet, and examining and eating it.

Looking for food helps satisfy a bird's natural curiosity. It gives the bird exercise, fun, and nutrition at the same time. In fact, finding food is probably the biggest challenge in a bird's life. For that reason, your bird will welcome a variety of foods.

While the pellets should be the main diet every day, treats are also appreciated. Small birds can have some seed as well as fruits such as apples, and vegetables such as lettuce, carrots, and corn. Make sure that any fruits and vegetables are washed well before serving them.

Larger birds love cracking open raw peanuts, almonds, and even walnuts. They enjoy picking raw corn right off the cob or holding a big chunk of apple or carrot in their foot and eating it. You can give them parrot seed mix once in a while as well. They will enjoy cracking open the sunflower and safflower seeds. Dried fruits and bananas are also very good.

Most pet stores carry seed sticks. You can hang them in the cage and let the bird work at pulling them apart. It's almost too easy to always have foods in a dish. Birds enjoy working to get their food. If you feed a bird this way, it will not only be healthy but it will have the enjoyment of finding new treats in its cage to discover, explore, and eat.

LIGHT

While a caged bird should never be left for long periods in direct hot sunlight, some amount of sun is good for the bird's health. If you live in a warm-weather climate, you may put your bird's cage in the sun for short periods of time. The ideal solution is having the cage half in sun, half in shade. If this is not possible, watch the bird carefully. If it begins to pant, get the cage out of the sun immediately.

Full-spectrum bird lights are available for indoor use. These lights emit the same light patterns as the rays from the sun, giving your birds needed exposure to ultraviolet light. These are the best lights to use for the overall health of your indoor birds.

WHY IS MY BIRD DOING THAT?

Look at Polly bobbing her head and neck at me. Isn't it cute?

Mitzy must really hate her food. Look how she's throwing her food around and sitting in her dish. Does she want a bath?

Ouch! Joey was sitting quietly on my shoulder when you came in— then he bit me on the ear. Bad bird!

There are reasons why a bird may bob its head and neck, throw all the food out of its food dish, or bite its favorite person. And it has nothing to do with being a good or bad bird.

Birds have not been popular pets for as long as dogs or cats. Their instincts are still closer to the wild state.

A bird bobbing its head and neck may be trying to regurgitate food from its crop. The crop is at the base of the neck and constantly supplies small amounts of food to the stomach. Food in the crop is undigested. It mixes with mucus and fluid. Mother birds feed their babies by regurgitating food.

And, believe it or not, your bird may be trying to feed you! Male budgies who are showing affection will regurgitate food.

They may do it to a favorite toy, into a mirror, or to their favorite person. Even the larger parrots may try to feed their owners as a sign of affection. Sometimes if you are showing affection to your bird, petting it around the head and neck, it will begin to regurgitate. Regurgitation from the crop is not vomiting.

How about Mitzy throwing all of her food out of the dish? It may be her favorite food, and she might still throw it out. Some mature females will get a very strong urge to go to nest. They want to breed. If there is no nest box attached to their cage, they look for a substitute. The food dish is the closest thing to a nest.

Birds like this may continue to look for a nesting spot in the cage. Lone females may sometimes even lay eggs. Remove them at once. If she persists in this behavior, she may be better off in a breeding program.

What about an unexpected bite? This is one reason some handlers feel that pet birds, especially larger parrots, should not be allowed to sit on your shoulder. A sudden bite to the ear or neck from a usually affectionate bird may not be an aggressive act toward you. On the contrary, it might be a protective one.

Suppose two birds are sitting side by side on a tree. Suddenly, one of them spots potential danger. It could be a bird of prey, another animal in the trees, or even humans. How does it warn the other bird, its friend or mate? It warns it by giving a sharp bite.

A sudden noise, a stranger coming into the room, or someone carrying a large object may prompt this behavior. Your bird perceives this as danger. Since you are its friend, it wants to warn

you. The sudden bite may hurt, but this doesn't mean it's a bad bird. If it does this too often, you may decide not to let it sit on your shoulder.

The trick to understanding your pet bird is to get to know it very well and also to learn more about bird behavior. The body language of a pet bird can tell you many things. You may misunderstand some behaviors unless you know about the bird's habits in the wild. You can learn by just watching and interacting with your bird. Here are a few more things to watch for:

You walk up to your bird, and it suddenly bows its head so low that it almost touches the perch it is sitting on. This is a common way for the bird to tell you it wants to be petted on the head and neck. If it did this to a companion in the wild, the other bird would preen it with its beak. That's the bird way of petting. The act of preening cleans and smooths the feathers. Birds will often preen themselves, but they love having another bird preen them as well.

Your bird suddenly begins pulling on your hair with its beak. It is simply preening you. It is not trying to hurt you. You are its companion, and your hair is your feathers. It just wants to make you feel and look good.

Your bird is sitting on its perch, relaxing. It may be standing on one leg, eyes closed. It seems to be going to sleep. Suddenly you hear it making a grinding noise with its beak. It may keep this up for quite some time. This is especially noticeable in larger birds. The bird is relaxing, but some believe that the grinding also keeps the lower beak sharp.

You look in the cage and notice that your bird looks thin. It has drawn its feathers very tight and stretched its body out. It has also stretched out its neck. This kind of body language indicates fear. Check around quickly and see what is frightening your bird.

It's summertime, and your bird is drawing its feathers tight but holding its wings away from its body. It is telling you that it's

too hot. Despite being warm-weather birds, hookbills, for example, suffer a great deal of stress in very hot and humid weather. If you see your bird holding its wings away from its body, try to cool it down. You can move it into an air-conditioned room (but not directly in front of the air conditioner). Or you can give it a cool shower with a spray bottle, such as a plant mister. Make sure that no chemicals have been in the bottle.

Your bird has spread its tail feathers wide apart. This flared tail is a sign of aggression. Other signs include flapping wings, hacking at the air with an open beak, and letting loose with a loud shriek. It may also fluff its feathers somewhat to make itself look bigger.

There are other quirky behaviors that you can look for in your bird: Some birds will allow their heads to be touched, but will bite if you try to touch them on the back. Others will only eat their food after they've tossed it to the cage floor. (No one said they couldn't be messy.)

HOW DO I GET MY BIRD TO DO THAT?

We have all seen pet birds on television or at a zoo doing tricks. Some talk on command. Others pull miniature wagons. Still others will pick up a ball and put it in a cup. These are advanced tricks that not all birds can learn, and not all owners can teach.

But everyone should be able to tame and train his or her bird to make it into a real pet. With some birds it is fairly easy. With others, it takes time and a lot a patience—and maybe a few Band-Aids to patch up the bites.

Left alone, all birds will develop a natural fear of humans. Others have that fear made worse by rough handling. This is especially true when birds are imported or smuggled into the country. But it can still happen with breeders who care only about the money they get for delivering birds to a pet shop or dealer.

Getting a bird to trust you is the first step toward being a good trainer . . . and a friend. This is easier with some birds than with others.

The younger the bird when you start training, the better. A budgie or cockatiel that has just been weaned (is eating on its own) can sometimes be hand-tamed in a day. It can take weeks, or sometimes longer, to tame an older bird.

If you get a hand-raised, hand-fed bird, it will be tame almost from the minute you bring it home. This is true even of the larger birds. But if you get an abused or neglected bird, it may have a fear of you, and especially of your hand.

To win a nervous bird's trust, start by offering its favorite food treat through the cage bars. Once it begins taking the food from your hand (and eating it, not throwing it down), you have accomplished the first step. Next you can begin putting your hand in the cage to offer the treat.

Once your bird learns that your hand will not hurt it, you can try to get it to sit on your hand. Put your hand gently up to the lower part of its chest and push slightly. Many trainers also

say "Up." If the bird steps up on your hand, you have done it. If not, keep trying. Don't work with the bird for too long or be too forceful. Talk quietly and don't allow anyone else in the room.

Once it is stepping on your hand, you can try to draw it out slowly. Or you can open the door and allow the bird to come out on its own. A tame bird will look forward to being out of the cage. A nervous or untamed bird will see the cage as its only safe haven.

TO CLIP OR NOT TO CLIP

Since it can fly, a bird's natural instinct is to get as high as it can to escape danger. If you allow an untamed bird out of the cage, the first thing it is going to do is fly to the highest place in the room. Then you may spend the rest of your training time chasing it. And if you lunge and grab the bird, you may get a very painful bite for your trouble. You'll also lose all the trust you have gained.

What is the solution? In this situation the best thing may be to have the bird's wings clipped. This will eliminate the possibility of the bird flying out an open window or door. Even the tamest bird, once outside, might decide it likes its freedom and will fly away.

Some owners allow tamed birds to fly in the house. They feel the exercise is important to the bird's health. But when you are taming, it's best to clip the wings (they'll grow back).

Wing clipping can be a frightening event for an untamed bird. It must be held by one person while its wings are cut by another. Done right, this will not hurt the bird at all. It might be best to have the vet do the clipping at first. Birds have excellent memories. If you clip the wings on a new bird, it may develop a distrust of you that will hamper your efforts to tame it.

Do not clip just one wing. This method can cause injury to the bird if it tries to fly. It will have almost no control of its movement. If you clip the primary feathers from both wings, you will keep the bird from gaining altitude. But it will have enough control to travel very short distances and to fly downward without free-falling.

Wing clipping serves two purposes. It make taming and training much easier, and it prevents escape. With its wings clipped, the bird cannot really fly away and will more often than not simply climb to the top of its cage when it comes out. You can work with your bird there or move it to a perch stand.

After your bird is tamed and does not fear you, you can decide whether to allow the wings to grow back or to keep them clipped. Just remember, a bird with clipped wings cannot have the ultimate accident: flying out an open door or window and disappearing.

Once your bird is stepping onto your hand, you can begin petting it around the head and neck. Most birds love to have their head and neck feathers stroked. It is better to pet opposite to the direction they grow or sideways to the growth. Be gentle. You can put one or two fingers down into the feathers, not just on the surface. You'll soon know what the bird likes best.

Before long your bird will look forward to climbing on your hand, coming out of the cage, and being petted. You can now begin walking around with it on your hand or forearm. If you don't mind the occasional nip, you can allow it on your shoulder.

When you put the bird back in its cage or on its perch, always say "Down!" This is the most important part of bird training. If the bird gets on and off your hand on command, you have established the trust and control that will let you teach it more.

Here are some of the most important bird-training tips:

1. Always be aware of your bird's moods and feelings.

2. *Never, never* hit your bird as punishment. A loud "No!" and quickly putting it back in its cage will do the trick. Birds will often meet violence with violence.

3. Do not grab and shake the bird's beak if it should bite you. This is the same as hitting the bird.

4. Do use food treats as a reward when training.

5. Never use a foot chain to keep the bird from flying. Clip the wings instead.

6. Go slowly. Let your bird dictate the length of your training sessions. Several shorter sessions are better than one long forced one.

7. Never make any quick movements. This can frighten the bird and really set you back. Speak quietly. Show your bird that you are relaxed and happy with it.

Training a bird is nothing at all like training a dog. Dogs have a natural instinct to please their owners, just as they would want to please the lead dog (or wolf) in a wild pack. Birds do not have this same instinct. Dogs also react well to some physical discipline. That's because in the wild they would be disciplined by the pack leader. Birds in the wild do not use this kind of physical aggression against each other. They are only aggressive with intruders.

So don't be an intruder. Be a trustworthy friend your bird wants to be with.

WHAT'S WRONG WITH MY BIRD?

With good care, a clean cage, the proper diet, enough exercise, and a bird or human companion, most pet birds will stay healthy for a long time. Birds are naturally hardy animals. But there are times when birds do get sick. It may be a simple cold or a serious bird disease.

It's not always easy to know when your bird isn't feeling well. In the wild, birds have a very strong instinct for survival. Since other animals can spot a sick bird quickly, and would make that bird its prey, birds have learned to hide any weakness. Because of this, birds will look completely normal while an illness is overtaking them. They show no outward sign of a disease until it is well advanced.

The sick pet bird in your home will behave in the same way as a bird in the wild. Therefore, you must be a kind of detective to spot an illness in its earliest stages. To do this, you must know your bird's "normal" behavior. Then you must watch for even the slightest change that would tell you something is wrong.

Here is a basic list of signs of illness to watch for:

1. Any change in eating and drinking habits. Birds digest food very quickly. That's why they eat on and off all day. If a bird stops eating, something is wrong.

2. Any kind of abnormal vomiting or regurgitation.

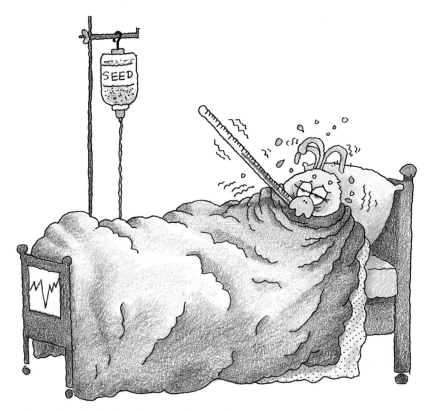

3. Any kind of discharge from the eyes or nose.

4. Any change in droppings. If droppings suddenly change color or become very watery or contain blood, your bird may be sick. Veterinarians will often test droppings to try to find what is wrong.

5. Any change in feathering. If the feathers begin looking ragged or torn, or if the bird is losing more feathers than normal.

6. Any change in the activity level or appearance: if the bird sits on the cage floor instead of a perch; if it appears tired

and listless; if it sleeps more than normal with its feathers fluffed and puffed; if it seems to be breathing heavily with its mouth open for long periods of time.

7. Any sign of lameness in a leg or droopiness in a wing.

8. Any sign of growths, swellings, or bumps on its body.

Cuts should not be treated lightly. Birds do not have a lot of blood in their bodies. When a small bird like a budgie loses just a few drops of blood, it can be serious. If you see a small cut, you must try to stop the bleeding immediately. You can get a special powder from the vet that will cause the blood to clot. Just press some of it on the wound. Cornstarch will also work. If the cut is large or the bleeding doesn't stop, get the bird to the vet fast.

You must also be aware of things in the home that can cause illness. A cage in direct sun or in a very hot, humid closed room can cause heatstroke. If your bird is out of the cage, don't let it get into any kind of household cleaner, solvent, or other poisonous substance.

The lungs of birds are very sensitive. Fumes from solvents or fuels can easily kill a bird. The fumes from some nonstick cooking appliances can also kill quickly if those appliances are allowed to overheat on the stove and begin to burn. Some houseplants are also poisonous to birds and should be kept out of reach.

Signs of poisoning include vomiting and diarrhea, sudden breathing problems, coughing, and perhaps even convulsions. If you see these sudden symptoms, call your veterinarian immediately.

FINDING A VETERINARIAN

Finding a good veterinarian to treat your bird isn't always easy. Not all veterinarians treat birds, and sometimes those who do admit that they aren't experts.

Before your bird becomes ill, call all the animal hospitals near your home and ask if the veterinarian treats birds. You should seek a vet who not only treats birds but who also keeps up on all the latest advances in avian medicine. So ask questions and keep the vet's phone number handy.

A sick bird is already under stress. A trip to the veterinarian is going to make the stress worse. All the more reason to find a good vet for your bird—one who knows how to keep your bird as calm as possible and isn't afraid of being bitten! Some vets will turn out the lights when examining a bird. They use a small flashlight during the initial examination. In the dark, the bird will remain much calmer and be less likely to bite.

People who love their pet birds want them to have long, happy, and healthy lives, and that means finding a vet who also loves birds.

IS THAT AN
EGG I SEE?

In the wild, birds will always mate and breed. This is how they keep the species going. As pets, birds will only breed if conditions are right.

Sometimes, however, a single female that wants to breed will begin laying eggs right in her cage. There is no chance, however, that the eggs will be fertile, because there is no male. You don't want your bird trying to sit on (incubate) the eggs. So in this case, simply remove the eggs as soon as they appear.

But what if you have a pair of birds that you want to breed? Then it is up to you to help them have babies (called chicks). What you need to do is attach a nest box to the cage. This may mean cutting the bars of the cage so they can get in and out of the box. If you don't want to do that, you'll need another cage that you can adapt.

The box must be the right size. It's easiest with small birds like budgies. They need a nest box that is only 5 inches (13 centimeters) long, 5 inches wide, and 7 inches (18 centimeters) high. Cockatiels need a box that is 12 inches (30 centimeters)

long, 12 inches wide, and 10 inches (25 centimeters) high. Large Amazon parrots need a box that is 14 inches (35 centimeters) long, 14 inches wide, and 24 inches (61 centimeters) high.

MALE OR FEMALE?

You have two blue crowned conures, or two blue-fronted Amazon parrots, or a pair of sulphur-crested cockatoos. They sit close together in their cage. They preen each other. They often look as if they're kissing. They must be male and female, you think. So you set up a nest box and . . . nothing happens.

True, some bonded pairs just won't breed. Maybe there is too much noise. Maybe they don't like people around. Maybe they just aren't in the mood. But there is something else. You might not have a male and female.

You can tell whether a budgie is male or female by the color of the cere above the beak. And you can tell if a cockatiel is male or female by whether it develops a yellow face. But with most other species it is often impossible to tell for sure whether the bird is male or female. Even longtime bird keepers have guessed wrong.

One way to know if a bird is male or female is to have its blood tested. You can also have a veterinarian do a simple surgical procedure in which the bird is examined with an instrument called an endoscope.

You may not want to go to the expense or put your birds through the stress of an operation. But if you are serious about breeding, you have to know the sex of your birds.

If your birds are willing, breeding can be easy. Budgies are good breeders and almost always make good parents. They feed their chicks until the babies are ready to eat on their own. Once the babies are weaned, they can be removed to their own cage.

Budgie eggs hatch in sixteen to eighteen days, and the chicks should be weaned and ready for new homes in four to five weeks. Larger birds take longer. For example, cockatiel eggs hatch in eighteen to twenty-one days, but the chicks usually aren't weaned for seven to nine weeks.

Amazon parrot and conure eggs hatch in twenty-four to twenty-eight days; the chicks are weaned between eight and fourteen weeks. The whole process takes a little longer for cockatoos and macaws.

Some experts say to hand-feed baby chicks from the very first day. But this is an around-the-clock job. For the home breeder, the general rule is to remove the babies at about four weeks and begin hand-feeding until they are weaned. This can be done with a special spoon or with large plastic syringes. Ask your vet to show you how to do this.

At four weeks, the chicks will be down to three or four feedings a day. You'll easily be able to see when the chick's crop is empty, and as you feed you will be able to see it fill. The chick will know when it has had enough.

As a rule, hand-fed babies make the sweetest pets. But a word of caution: A hand-fed baby can sometimes become very demanding. Baby birds get food by begging. It's a natural instinct. Soon your hand-fed baby will beg food from you. It will also expect a lot of attention, and will beg for that, too, even after it is weaned. New owners must be careful not to give the bird more attention during its first few weeks at home than they will be able or willing to give it later. If you lavish affection on your bird for a month, then forget it, you will have an unhappy, noisy, and perhaps aggressive bird.

If you breed your birds at home, follow these few rules:

1. Always keep a record of when eggs are laid and when the chicks hatch. You'll know what to expect and when, and the record will be useful for future reference.

2. If the chicks are in the nest box, use wood shavings or paper toweling as a bed. Change it frequently. This will absorb droppings and keep the chicks' feet and legs clean.

3. Handle the chicks very gently. They are extremely fragile.

4. If you remove them to hand-feed, they must be kept warm, at about 85°F (29°C). This can be done by putting them in an empty aquarium on top of a heating pad. A special heating lamp for baby chicks can also be used.

5. Parent birds should be fed a very high-quality diet when breeding and feeding. Some pellet companies make a special

breeding food with a slightly higher level of protein than the regular feed.

6. If you hand-feed, get a commercial food for chicks. It can be supplemented with a baby-food vegetable mix and perhaps some natural applesauce.

7. Food that dribbles onto the beak and body of the chick must be wiped off with a warm, damp towel. Dried food can cause sores on the skin and deformities to the still-soft beak.

8. Watch for signs that the parents are not feeding the chicks. This will happen once in a while. Then you must begin hand-feeding immediately.

Breeding your birds can be an exciting and educational experience. But like every other phase of bird keeping, learn all you can first. Talk to the experts. If you are not sure about something, ask. You have little lives depending on you.

FIND OUT MORE

Bremmer. *How Birds Live.* Tulsa: EDC Publishing, 1981.

Forsyth, Adrian, and Laurel Aziz. *Exploring the World of Birds: An Equinox Guide to Avian Life.* Buffalo: Firefly Books, 1990.

Hornblow, Leonora and Arthur. *Birds Do the Strangest Things.* New York: Random House Books for Young Readers, 1991.

Jameson, Pam, and Tina Hearne. *Responsible Pet Care Series.* Vero Beach, FL: Rourke Publications, 1989.

McPherson, Mark. *Choosing Your Pet.* Mahwah, NJ: Troll Associates, 1985.

INDEX

African gray parrots, 15, 21
Alexander the Great, 13–14
Alexandrine parakeets, 13
Amazon parrots, 14, 21, 55, 57
Aviculture, 14

Behavior, 35–40
Biting, 36–37
Body language, 37–40
Breeding, 10, 54–61
Bringing home, 22–25
Budgerigars (parakeets), 13–14,
    17–18, 54, 57

Cages, 28–29
Canaries, 14
Cere, 17, 56
Chewing, 31
Chicks, 54, 57–61
Chinese (ancient), 13
Cockatiels, 14, 18–19, 54, 56, 57

Cockatoos, 14, 21
Conures, 14, 57
Crop, 35
Cuts, 51

Dinosaurs, 13
Domestically raised birds, 15, 16
Drafts, 25
Droppings, 50

Endoscope, 57
Extinction, 16

Finches, 14
Food, 25, 32–34, 59–60
Fruits, 32–34

Grinding, 38

Illness, 23, 48–53
Imported birds, 15–16, 41

Life spans, 14, 18, 20, 25
Light, 34
Lovebirds, 14, 20
Lutino cockatiels, 18

Macaws, 14, 21
Memories, 16, 44

Nest box, 36, 54–55
Night covering, 25
Nuts, 34

Parakeets (see Budgerigars)
Parrots, 14–16, 21–22, 55, 57
Pearl cockatiels, 15
Pellets, 32, 33
Perches, 30–31
Petting, 38, 44, 45
Pheasants, 13
Pied cockatiels, 18
Poisoning, 51

Preening, 38
Prehistoric animals, 13
Psittacine family, 14

Regurgitation, 35–36

Second bird, 27
Seeds, 32–34
Sex, 17, 56–57
Smuggling, 16, 41
Stress, 23–24, 53

Talking, 11, 14, 17–19, 21
Taming and training, 14, 18, 41–47
Toys, 31–32
Trust, 41–43

Vegetables, 32–34
Veterinarians, 52–53, 57

Wing clipping, 43–44, 46